OXFORD FREE PUBLIC LIBRARY
339 MAIN STREET
OXFORD, MA 01540

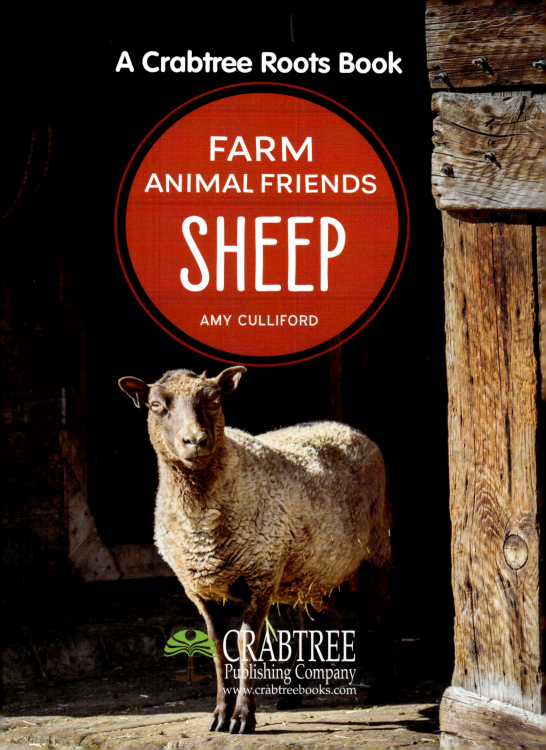

A Crabtree Roots Book

FARM ANIMAL FRIENDS
SHEEP

AMY CULLIFORD

CRABTREE
Publishing Company
www.crabtreebooks.com

School-to-Home Support for Caregivers and Teachers

This book helps children grow by letting them practice reading. Here are a few guiding questions to help the reader with building his or her comprehension skills. Possible answers appear here in red.

Before Reading:
- What do I think this book is about?
    - *This book is about sheep.*
    - *This book is about sheep on farms.*

- What do I want to learn about this topic?
    - *I want to learn what sound a sheep makes.*
    - *I want to learn what colors sheep can be.*

During Reading:
- I wonder why…
    - *I wonder why some sheep are different colors.*
    - *I wonder why some sheep have horns.*

- What have I learned so far?
    - *I have learned that sheep live on farms.*
    - *I have learned that sheep can be big or little.*

After Reading:
- What details did I learn about this topic?
    - *I have learned that some sheep have horns.*
    - *I have learned that sheep can be different colors.*

- Read the book again and look for the vocabulary words.
    - *I see the word **farm** on page 5 and the word **horns** on page 12. The other vocabulary words are found on page 14.*

These sheep are on a **farm**.

Some sheep are big.

Some sheep are little.

Sheep can be white, brown, or black.

Some sheep have **horns**.

All sheep say, *baa!*

Word List
Sight Words

a	brown	say
all	can	some
are	is	these
be	little	this
big	on	white
black	or	

Words to Know

farm **horns** **sheep**

33 Words

This is a **sheep**.

These sheep are on a **farm**.

Some sheep are big.

Some sheep are little.

Sheep can be white, brown, or black.

Some sheep have **horns**.

All sheep say, *baa*!

Written by: Amy Culliford
Designed by: Rhea Wallace
Series Development: James Earley
Proofreader: Kathy Middleton
Educational Consultant: Christina Lemke M.Ed.

Photographs:
Shutterstock: NPDstock: cover (tl); Menna: cover (tr); Laurinson Crusoe: cover (b); Amy K. Mitchell p. 1; Pete Pahham: p. 3, 14; Zane Vergara: p. 4, 14; Natelle: p. 7; Alexey Stiop: p. 9; FooTToo: p. 10-11; wk1003mike: p. 12; fotorauschen: p. 13

Library and Archives Canada Cataloguing in Publication
Title: Sheep / Amy Culliford.
Names: Culliford, Amy, 1992- author.
Description: Series statement: Farm animal friends | "A Crabtree roots book".
Identifiers: Canadiana (print) 20200382500 | Canadiana (ebook) 20200382519 | ISBN 9781427134554 (hardcover) | ISBN 9781427132505 (softcover) | ISBN 9781427132567 (HTML)
Subjects: LCSH: Sheep—Juvenile literature.
Classification: LCC SF375.2 .C85 2021 | DDC j636.3—dc23

Library of Congress Cataloging-in-Publication Data
Names: Culliford, Amy, 1992- author.
Title: Sheep / Amy Culliford.
Description: New York : Crabtree Publishing Company, 2021. | Series: Farm animal friends : a Crabtree roots book | Includes index. | Audience: Ages 4-6 | Audience: Grades K-1 | Summary: "Early readers are introduced to sheep and life on a farm. Simple sentences accompany engaging pictures"-- Provided by publisher.
Identifiers: LCCN 2020049889 (print) | LCCN 2020049890 (ebook) | ISBN 9781427134554 (hardcover) | ISBN 9781427132505 (paperback) | ISBN 9781427132567 (ebook)
Subjects: LCSH: Sheep--Juvenile literature. | Livestock--Juvenile literature.
Classification: LCC SF375.2 .C85 2021 (print) | LCC SF375.2 (ebook) | DDC 636.3--dc23
LC record available at https://lccn.loc.gov/2020049889
LC ebook record available at https://lccn.loc.gov/2020049890

Crabtree Publishing Company
www.crabtreebooks.com   1-800-387-7650

Printed in the U.S.A./022021/CG20201130

Copyright © 2021 **CRABTREE PUBLISHING COMPANY**

All rights reserved. No part of this publication may be reproduced, stored in a retrieval system or be transmitted in any form or by any means, electronic, mechanical, photocopying, recording, or otherwise, without the prior written permission of Crabtree Publishing Company. In Canada: We acknowledge the financial support of the Government of Canada through the Canada Book Fund for our publishing activities.

Published in the United States
Crabtree Publishing
347 Fifth Avenue, Suite 1402-145
New York, NY, 10016

Published in Canada
Crabtree Publishing
616 Welland Ave.
St. Catharines, Ontario L2M 5V6

OXFORD FREE PUBLIC LIBRARY
339 MAIN STREET
OXFORD, MA 01540